SCALY BABIES

REPTILES GROWING UP

GINNY JOHNSTON AND JUDY CUTCHINS

SCALY BABIES

REPTILES GROWING UP

MORROW JUNIOR BOOKS

NEW YORK

PHOTO CREDITS

Permission for the following photographs is gratefully acknowledged: Ken Fahey, Auburn University, Department of Zoology, pp. 2, 3; Gregory C. Greer, pp. 7 (bottom), 24, 26; Steven W. Ruckel, p. 22; Win Seyle, pp. 25, 27, 37; Lawrence A. Wilson, pp. 13, 32, 33. All other photographs by Judy Cutchins.

Printed in Italy.

HC   3 4 5 6 7 8 9 10

PA 1 2 3 4 5 6 7 8 9 10

Library of Congress Cataloging-in-Publication Data
Johnston, Ginny.
Scaly babies.
Includes index.
Summary: Describes the physical characteristics and behavior of a variety of baby reptiles as they struggle to survive and grow to adulthood.
1. Reptiles—Development—Juvenile literature.
[1. Reptiles] I. Cutchins, Judy. II. Title.
QL644.2.J64 1988   597.9'0439   87-18599
ISBN 0-688-07305-0
ISBN 0-688-07306-9 (lib. bdg.)
ISBN 0-688-09998-X (pbk.)

ACKNOWLEDGMENTS

We wish to thank the members of the herpetology department at Zoo Atlanta, Atlanta, Georgia, for their help in the development of *Scaly Babies.* We were fortunate in having both the staff and the outstanding reptile collection available for our research. At Zoo Atlanta, Dennis Herman and Greg George were tirelessly patient with our questions and observations. Because of them we have greater respect not only for the reptiles, but also for the scientists who study them.

We thank the following specialists for their expert comments on our text: Susan Barnard, Greg George, Dennis Herman, and Howard Hunt of Zoo Atlanta; Steve Ruckel of the Georgia Department of Natural Resources; Win Seyle of the Savannah Science Museum, Savannah, Georgia; Bern Tryon at the Knoxville Zoo, Knoxville, Tennessee; Greg Greer and Ken Fahey of the Georgia Herpetological Society; and Larry Wilson of Fernbank Science Center in Atlanta. Their comments ensure the accuracy of our book. Special thanks go to Larry Wilson, Win Seyle, Greg Greer, Steve Ruckel, and Ken Fahey for the use of their photographs; and to Dennis Bryant for allowing us to photograph his newborn emerald tree boas.

Finally, we want to express our appreciation to Andrea Curley, our friend and editor at William Morrow. She continues to encourage and support our endeavors.

Without all these people, *Scaly Babies* would not have been possible.

CONTENTS

REPTILES AND THEIR BABIES

For many people, the word "reptile" describes an ugly, slippery, and sometimes dangerous animal. But reptiles are not slimy, and most are not dangerous. There are nearly six thousand different kinds of these scaly-skinned animals in the world today. It is true that some are large and scary-looking and a few are venomous, but most reptiles are harmless to humans. Like many wild animals, reptiles may strike or bite to defend themselves. But they rarely bother a person who has not disturbed or startled them.

Every reptile has a role in the balance of nature. Many have roles that are helpful to people. Some reptiles, especially snakes and lizards, eat insects, rats, and other animals that can be pests.

A reptile's life usually begins inside an eggshell. The warmth of the sun incubates the eggs so they will hatch. Each hatchling has a horny tip on its top jaw that helps it break out of the egg. After a few days, this "egg tooth" falls off. Usually the newborn reptile looks like a tiny copy of its parents. Only the color or pattern of its skin may be different.

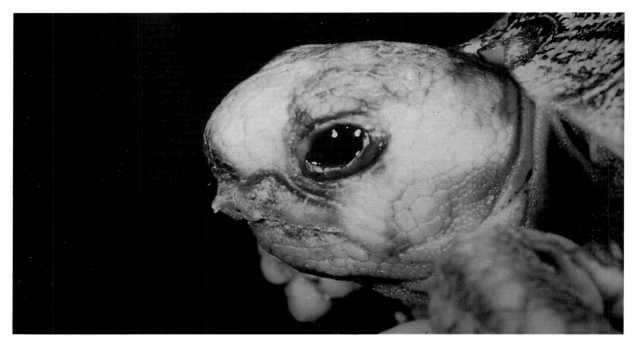

This gopher tortoise is just a few hours old and still has its tiny egg tooth. In a day or two, the horny tip will dry up and fall off.

From the moment of hatching, most reptiles are on their own. They do not need to learn how to take care of themselves. Each is born with instincts to hide, escape from enemies, and find food. But a baby reptile's tiny size is a big problem. Reptiles are often food for other animals. A little reptile faces the danger of being eaten by mammals, birds of prey, and larger reptiles.

Extreme hot or cold temperatures can be deadly for a reptile. During such weather, reptiles go underground and are inactive. In many parts of the world, reptiles remain out of sight during the cold months of winter. With warmer temperatures, animals become active once again.

One of the best ways for a young reptile to protect itself from all

An eight-inch-long black racer snake escapes from its soft, leathery eggshell.

kinds of dangers is to hide in a sheltered place. Even in warm weather, young reptiles spend many hours each day hidden from their enemies and from uncomfortable temperatures. But they cannot stay hidden all the time. The need for food brings them out of their hiding places.

Reptiles of any size must be aware of danger at all times. Many baby reptiles survive only because of their amazing instincts.

Scaly Babies: Reptiles Growing Up describes the lives and instincts of some typical reptile babies as they struggle to survive. The babies presented are particularly colorful and interesting examples of the variety of reptiles throughout the world.

1

BABY SNAKES

Most snakes lay soft, leathery-shelled eggs. Others do not lay eggs. The mother boa constrictor, for example, keeps the developing young inside her body until it is time to give birth.

A newborn snake's body is covered with dry, waterproof scales, just like those of an adult snake. These tough scales protect the little snake from scrapes and cuts as it slithers over rocks or rough ground. The scales along the underside of a snake's body are called scutes. These scales are longer and wider than the others. The front edge of each scute is loose. The snake's ribs and strong muscles push the scutes against the ground. The edges catch on uneven places and anchor the snake as it pulls itself along.

A snake cannot shut its eyes because it does not have any eyelids. Each eye is covered and protected by a round, clear scale called a spectacle. As a snake grows, it sheds the outside layer of its scales. The spectacle scales are the first ones to break loose. Several days later, the rest of the outside layer is loose. The snake wiggles out, head first, and leaves its shed skin turned inside out.

All snakes have sharp teeth for grabbing and holding their prey. Since they do not have any teeth for chewing, snakes must swallow their food whole. Snakes that have venom have two extra teeth called fangs. The fangs are often larger and longer than the other teeth. Throughout their lives, snakes grow new teeth to replace lost or broken ones.

This young indigo snake will soon be shedding its skin. The spectacle scales covering the eyes look cloudy when they loosen from the new scales underneath.

ASIAN COBRA

In the soft, rotten wood at the base of a tree stump, a female cobra laid twenty eggs. The leathery eggs were left alone to develop in the warm Asian sunshine. Inside each eggshell, a forming baby floated in a clear sac of water. A yolk provided food for the developing cobra.

After sixty days, the baby snake was fully formed and most of the yolk was gone. The cobras began to hatch. Using an egg tooth to open the eggshell, the first hatching cobra slit an opening large enough for its body to slip through. The tiny baby pushed its head out. Its forked tongue flicked in and out, sensing the odors in the air for the first time. A whole day passed before the ten-inch-long baby slithered from its egg. Its new scales were wet and slippery. But the scales soon dried, and the cobra was smooth and shiny.

The hatchling had moved just a foot from the nest when a large bird landed nearby. Already the tiny cobra had the instincts of its parents. Hissing loudly, the hatchling raised the front of its body straight up and flared its neck "hood" out in a dangerous-looking pose. The startled bird flew away. Just a few minutes old, the baby cobra was ready to defend itself against any enemy.

Little cobras have a different personality from that of their parents. The youngsters strike at everything that startles them. The adults, fortunately, are much more shy. The bite of an adult cobra could kill a person. The cobra's venom glands secrete a deadly poison into the wound. A baby cobra's bite is venomous, too, but it would probably not cause a person to die. The venom of the baby is, however, deadly to mice and other animals that are its prey. There is enough venom in the bite of a five-week-old Asian cobra to kill an adult mouse in two and a half minutes.

Cobras do not live in the United States. In Asia, India, and Africa,

(Right)
When a bright light is held close to the eggshell, the blood vessels of a developing snake inside can be seen.

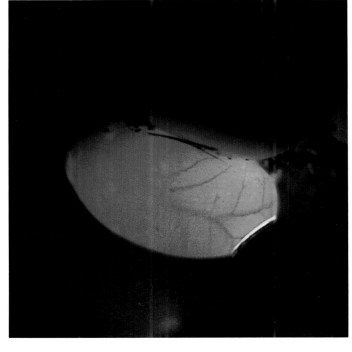

(Below)
A baby cobra instinctively spreads its hood and prepares to strike in the same way an adult cobra would. Although its fangs are small, the baby's venom is dangerous.

these dangerous snakes are found in jungles and in people's yards and gardens. Like all reptiles, cobras are an important part of their habitat. These predators help keep nature in balance. They eat rats, mice, frogs, birds, other snakes, and even fish. Their diet helps keep the numbers of those animals from growing too large. Sometimes the hunter cobras become the hunted animals. Big owls, eagles, mongooses, and wild boars eat all kinds of snakes, including cobras.

This cobra has smooth, glossy scales after shedding its outer skin.

Just a few hours old, the baby boa explores some of the shrubs and trees of the tropical rain forest.

EMERALD TREE BOA

With its strong, muscular body, the baby emerald tree boa had climbed easily through the bushes and low tree limbs only minutes after it was born. Its prehensile tail helped the youngster grasp the branches. Now the baby boa hangs on a low branch. Its sixteen-inch-long orange body is looped into a fist-shaped bundle.

Nearby, the mother boa constrictor rests after giving birth to twelve colorful, healthy babies. Some of the babies are orange and others are green. At first the young boas explore close by. In a few hours, they will all go their separate ways.

The little orange baby resting in the tree blends well with the branches. Its brothers and sisters are hidden among the leaves. This camouflage is the best protection for such small animals in the South American rain forest. A newborn boa can protect itself only by hiding. Its sharp teeth are still tiny, and its jaws are not yet strong. In a few years, the emerald boa will grow to a length of five feet and will have teeth almost one half inch long.

The mother boa did not lay white, shelled eggs like the cobra. Instead, the young developed inside her body for 240 days. While developing, each little boa was inside its own clear, water-filled sac. A yellow yolk inside each of the sacs provided food for the growing baby. Each snake was born when its birth sac was pushed out of the mother's body by her powerful muscles. The sacs slid out one by one, through an opening, called a vent, between the mother's belly scales

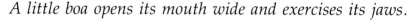

A little boa opens its mouth wide and exercises its jaws.

Even though some of the baby boas are orange, their scales will gradually change to the beautiful green color of their parents'.

near her tail. In a short time, each baby broke free of its birth sac and faced the world of the jungle for the first time.

As months go by, the young boa will grow and shed the old, top layer of scales often. Its orange color will turn an emerald green like that of its beautiful mother and father.

As it grows older, the young emerald tree boa will be an important hunter in the jungle. Although it is not venomous, the boa helps keep nature in balance by eating lizards, birds, monkeys, and other snakes. It is a constrictor snake and kills its prey by squeezing it with powerful muscles.

BABY LIZARDS

Lizards may be found racing across the ground, climbing trees, or burrowing underground. Many are active during the day. Others, especially those that live in the desert, move around in the cool of the night or at dawn.

A few kinds of lizards give birth to live young, but most lay eggs. The mother lizards hide their eggs carefully in sand or soft soil where the sun will warm them. As soon as the eggs hatch, lizard babies are ready to care for themselves. Growing quickly on a diet of insects, spiders, and worms, most young lizards are adult-size by the end of their second summer.

Lizards are truly the escape artists of the reptile world. Besides great speed, some have an amazing ''breakaway'' tail. When a lizard is attacked by a predator, part of the lizard's tail ''pops'' off, and the broken piece twitches on the ground. When the predator stops to investigate, the lizard escapes to safety. Within a few weeks, the lizard regrows the end of its tail. The new tail is not quite as long as the old one, and it may not be quite the same color.

Two kinds of lizards have another way of defending themselves. The beaded lizards of Mexico and the Gila monster of the American Southwest do not drop off their tails when disturbed. These lizards have venom and powerful jaws. Since they are not fast runners, a venomous bite is important for their survival.

This five-lined lizard is one of the speedy escape artists of the lizard world.

GILA MONSTER

A desert in the southwestern United States is a busy place at night. Reptiles and other animals that hide during the heat of the summer day come out to find food. As the six-inch-long hatchling Gila monster crawls from its hiding place among the rocks, it moves with care. The baby lizard could be eaten by owls or snakes.

The baby Gila searches for insects by touching its tongue to the ground and "tasting" for an insect's scent. When it senses an insect nearby, the lizard lunges quickly, grabs the prey, and holds it tightly with very sharp teeth. When the little Gila chews, venom seeps from its bottom jaw into the bite marks on the insect. Soon the prey is still. The Gila monster drags the lifeless body under a rock and munches it.

Rarely seen in the daytime, a Gila monster hides in rocky crevices or sandy burrows. At night, it searches for eggs and small animals to eat.

Although deadly to an insect, the baby Gila's teeth could not easily pierce the skin of a person. The two-foot-long adult Gila lizard has much more powerful jaws, and its bite would be dangerous to a human. Even though the venom is strong, the Gila's name of "monster" is really unfair. The Gila monster is a very peaceful lizard. It attacks only prey and bites people only in self-defense.

The baby Gila hatched from an egg its mother buried in the sand. There were three eggs in this mother Gila's nest. Each two-inch-long egg was soft, white, and leathery, like a snake egg. The Gila monster's eggs incubated for about five months. After hatching, the baby was on its own immediately.

A Gila monster uses its tiny egg tooth to slit open the leathery eggshell. With just its head showing, the lizard may wait several hours before climbing all the way out.

The young Gila monster has bumpy, beadlike scales all over the top and sides of its body. Like all reptile scales, they are dry and waterproof. The scales protect the animal from losing too much of its body's moisture in the desert heat. A baby Gila monster often spends the hot daytime hours safely hidden in the burrows of other animals.

The Gila does not have a breakaway tail as many lizards do. It uses its thick tail to store extra fat for nourishment. During the winter months, the Gila monster will live in an underground burrow. Its heart rate and breathing will slow down. The Gila will not grow much during the winter, and it will use only a little of the fat stored in its tail.

If a baby Gila survives the harsh desert conditions and escapes predators, it may grow to be two feet long and weigh four pounds. Adult Gila monsters are among the largest lizards in the United States.

This young Gila could live for several months on the fat stored in its tail.

3 BABY CROCODILIANS

Alligators, crocodiles, gharials, and caimans belong to a group of reptiles called the crocodilians. A baby crocodilian looks very much like a lizard, except that its skin is tougher and the scales are larger. Most lizards live on dry land, while the crocodilians spend much of their time in the water. Like the adults, hatchlings have webbed back feet and flattened tails for swimming.

A female crocodilian usually makes a nest mound of soil. She digs a hole in the mound and lays her eggs. For seventy or eighty days, the mother stays near her nest and defends it against egg-eating predators. After many weeks, the watchful mother hears her young call within the nest as they begin to hatch. She scrapes away the soil that covers them. Gently she carries her youngsters in her mouth from the nest to the nearby water. She opens her mouth and releases the babies. They instinctively know how to swim. Most hatchling crocodilians stay near their mothers for many months.

Like other crocodilians, these dwarf caiman babies were carried to the water in their mother's jaws.

Newborn crocodilians are less than twelve inches long. On a diet of tadpoles, insects, and small fish, they grow rapidly. Crocodilians continue to grow throughout their entire lives. As they get older, their growth rate slows down. Some adult crocodiles are nearly twenty feet long. Crocodilians are usually the largest predators in their habitats. By eating some of the ducks, turtles, fish, and snakes, the crocodilians help keep nature in balance.

AMERICAN ALLIGATOR

   With webbed back feet tucked close to its body, the nine-inch-long baby alligator floated along in the shallow water of Georgia's Okefenokee Swamp. Only its eyes and nose appeared above the surface as it swam silently through the water. Then, with hardly a ripple, the two-week-old alligator sank beneath the surface in search of food. Its knife-shaped tail sliced quickly back and forth as the baby chased tadpoles and minnows. Capturing a minnow, the little alligator held its prey between its jaws with dozens of needlelike teeth. Then the alligator came to the surface to eat. Throwing back its head and gulping down the minnow without chewing, the baby finished its meal in just a few seconds.

Alligators are excellent swimmers even when they are only a few minutes old.

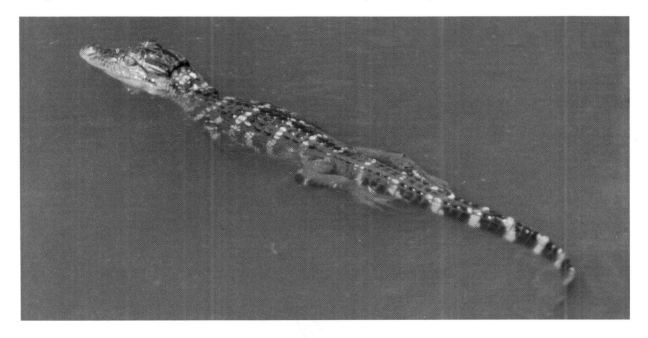

An alligator tosses its head back and swallows its food without chewing.

After eating, the young alligator crawled onto the bank to lie in the warm sunshine. Basking in the sun is very important for cold-blooded reptiles. Being cold-blooded does not really mean their blood is cold. It means that the temperature inside the animal's body is changed by the temperature of the air around the animal. Moving into the shade or going for a swim cools the alligator's body before it gets too hot. Reptiles must be careful not to overheat.

Black and yellow bands of scales camouflage the youngster, helping it blend in with sunlight and shadows on the bank. Its enemies, such as large water birds, snapping turtles, and sometimes other alligators, cannot see the baby easily. Unlike many other reptiles, a hatchling

*After basking in the summer sunshine,
this alligator cools off in the swamp.*

alligator has a very unusual means of protection—its mother is never far away. If frightened, a youngster gives a loud *"ee-yurk! ee-yurk!"* cry, and the mother alligator swims quickly to investigate. She sometimes answers her baby's call with a loud hiss. The nine-foot-long mother certainly scares away most of the baby's enemies. Unfortunately, with more than thirty babies, it is impossible for her to protect them all.

Predators often snap up baby alligators in spite of the mother's protective instincts.

The young alligator will remain near its mother for the first two years of its life. It will have fewer and fewer enemies as it grows to be the largest reptile in the United States, reaching lengths of twelve feet or more.

This newly hatched alligator is just nine inches long. The black and yellow bands of scales that camouflage it will turn almost solid black as the alligator grows.

4

BABY TURTLES

Most turtles fit into one of three groups: sea turtles, freshwater turtles, and land turtles. Land turtles are sometimes known as tortoises. Turtles are different from all other reptiles. Except for a few types of turtles with leathery shells, these reptiles have hard, bony shells that protect their bodies. The shell that covers the top of many land turtles is tall and dome-shaped. Some land turtles can close themselves up inside their shells because the part of the shell beneath the body is hinged and can snap tightly closed against the top. Water turtles are unable to close themselves up like this. Their shells are not domed and are streamlined for swimming.

Like many reptiles, every turtle hatches from an egg carefully buried in the ground by its mother. Mother turtles do not stay to protect the nest or care for hatchlings. A baby turtle hatches with its shell fully formed. The new shell is soft and tender. Often a hatchling stays buried in the nest area while its shell dries and hardens. The youngster is nourished by the remaining yolk sac, which is still attached to its bottom shell. The outside layer of a turtle's shell is made of thin, horny scales called scutes. The number of scutes never changes, but the size of each one does. As a young turtle's scutes grow, the shell gets larger. It will take several years for a hatchling's shell to grow big enough and thick enough to protect the little turtle from its enemies.

Summer is hatching time for water turtles of all kinds.

LOGGERHEAD SEA TURTLE

Moonlight sparkled on the waves as a three-hundred-pound loggerhead sea turtle pulled her enormous body onto the South Carolina beach. Instinctively she found a nesting place in the sand far from the water. The mother turtle dug a hole over a foot deep with her clawed back flippers. She laid a hundred round, soft-shelled eggs in the light-bulb-shaped nest. After scraping sand over the eggs, the giant mother lumbered back to the ocean, never to see her youngsters. Loggerheads have been nesting in this way since the days of the dinosaurs.

A female loggerhead sea turtle comes out of the sea only at nesting time. She may come onto the beach to lay eggs several times in the same summer.

Tremendous numbers of sea turtle eggs never hatch. Nests are destroyed by storms or extra-high tides. Other nests are attacked by hungry raccoons, wild pigs, or ghost crabs. But this nest remained undisturbed. Incubated by the summer sun, the eggs hatched in sixty days. On a star-filled night, the young turtles scrambled up and out of the sand together. The hatchling loggerheads were only one and one-quarter inches long.

These little turtles were lucky: they found their way to the ocean. Instinct led them in the direction of the light sparkling on the waves. The beach where they hatched was a deserted one. No hotel or car lights confused the babies and caused them to head in the wrong direction. On beaches that are built up with houses and streets, some hatchlings die because they never make it to the ocean.

On a summer evening, hatchling turtles race instinctively toward the ocean. Each is alone once it reaches the water's edge.

With extra-long flippers, this hatchling will be able to "fly" through the water.

Although they seem too tiny and lightweight to swim against the waves, hatchling loggerheads are very strong swimmers. Diving into the pounding waves, they head out to sea. Separated from one another in the deep water, the tiny babies are on their own. They find patches of seaweed drifting in the water. Here they hide and find tiny insect-sized sea animals to eat. Carried along by ocean currents, little sea turtles may travel thousands of miles in their first years of life.

Because of the danger of being eaten by large fish and other sea predators, only one hatchling in a thousand survives to become an adult turtle. If a young loggerhead makes it to adulthood, it may live as long as a hundred years!

SNAPPING TURTLE

The little snapping turtle grasps a cricket tightly in its mouth. Although turtles have no teeth, the hatchling snapper has a powerful set of jaws with a sharp, cutting edge. With long front claws, the one-month-old baby tugs at its meal, tearing the cricket into bite-sized pieces. After eating, the tiny snapper settles onto the muddy pond bottom. Four months earlier, the mother snapper had dug her nest in soft, dry ground forty feet from the water. After digging the nest and laying thirty eggs, she left.

Once caught, an adult snapper's prey cannot escape the turtle's powerful jaws.

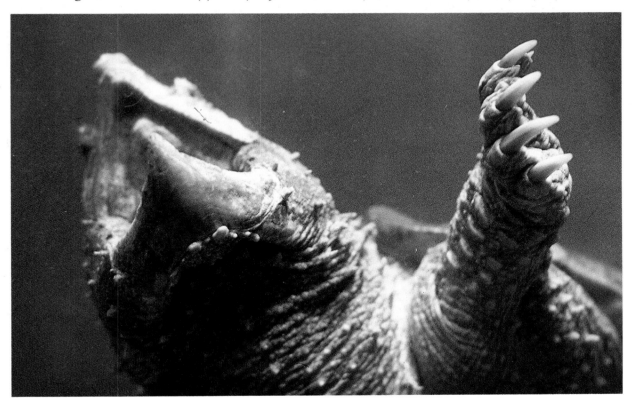

The unusually long tail of a baby snapper makes this little turtle easy to recognize.

On a warm August day, the little snapper was the first in the nest to hatch. The job of breaking free from its tough eggshell had not been an easy one. The snapper, like most reptiles and birds, grew a small, horny point on the end of its top jaw while still inside the eggshell. This little egg tooth was used to make a slit in the eggshell. After many hours of work, the little turtle faced the world for the first time. After a few days, the egg tooth fell off. The baby's long tail and ragged-shaped shell looked very much like those of the adult snapping turtle, but the baby was much, much tinier. The hatchling's body was just two inches long, with a two-inch tail. An adult snapper may weigh over thirty pounds and become bigger around than a dinner plate. Its tail is as long as its body.

For the first few days, the hatchling had a yolk sac still attached, so it needed no additional food. After a week, the yolk supply was used up and the little snapper left the nest. Instinctively it headed for the pond nearby.

While an adult snapping turtle has no natural enemies, a baby snapper must watch out for everything. Birds, fish, bullfrogs, snakes, and larger turtles can swallow a hatchling, shell and all. The young turtle must eat to grow. It has to risk predators to find a steady supply of insects, tadpoles, and minnows for food.

For several days after hatching, the leftover yolk sac is gradually absorbed as it provides food for the tiny snapping turtle.

Blending in with the pond's muddy bottom, the hatchling snapper hides from its enemies as well as its prey.

Snappers do not climb out onto rocks and logs to bask in the sun as often as other water turtles. They spend much of each day resting in the mud. Snappers are active at night, creeping along the pond bottom snapping up crayfish and leeches. During its first year, the tiny snapping turtle will spend most of its time on the muddy pond bottom, where it is well camouflaged. By the end of the year, the baby snapper's body size will increase by an inch and its shell will grow tougher and thicker. As it grows larger, the baby will have fewer enemies. In fifteen years, the little snapper will become one of the biggest of freshwater turtles. Common snapping turtles are found in quiet, mud-bottom ponds throughout the eastern United States.

GOPHER TORTOISE

Seven tiny hatchling gopher tortoises pushed up and out of their sandy nest. Each dug through the soil with the soft claws on its sturdy little front legs. The baby turtles gulped the hot, muggy air of early September. Sand stuck to their beautifully patterned shells and hid some of their bright yellow color.

After incubating for one hundred days, a tiny gopher tortoise breaks free of its shell.

A gopher tortoise's burrow may also be the hiding place for frogs, lizards, rabbits, burrowing owls, and snakes.

The nest was in a pile of sand at the entrance of their mother's tunnel. Like every adult gopher tortoise, the female had used her broad, powerful front feet to dig a twenty-foot-long tunnel, or burrow, in which to live. In early summer, the mother tortoise had laid her eggs. After covering them, she paid no more attention to her nest, even though she crawled past it as she entered and left her burrow each day.

One hundred days later, the little gopher tortoises hatched. After resting a few hours, the hatchlings wandered off in separate directions. Like the adult, a baby gopher tortoise digs a burrow in which to rest and hide. Its first tunnel is only a foot or two long and about as big around as a golf ball.

On mornings when the weather is good, the hatchling trudges out slowly in search of food. A gopher tortoise is a plant eater. With a scissorlike motion of its tiny jaws, the baby tortoise easily chomps through the tender parts of grass, or the ripe red fruits of the cactus. These foods also provide water the tortoise needs to live in sandy coastal areas of the southeastern United States.

The baby gopher tortoise often returns to the cool, shady burrow in the middle of each day. While the burrow protects the hatchling from the sun's heat, it does not hide the young tortoise from enemies. Indigo snakes and skunks are known to eat tender hatchlings. These animals often seek the shelter of adult gopher tortoise burrows. Skunks

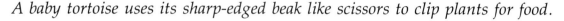

A baby tortoise uses its sharp-edged beak like scissors to clip plants for food.

In about eighteen years, this golf-ball-sized hatchling gopher tortoise will grow as big as its basketball-sized mother.

and raccoons have strong claws. They can dig into sandy soil and make a quick meal of any reptile eggs or hatchlings that they find. Sensing danger, a baby gopher tortoise can pull its head and tail into its shell. Its tough, scaly front legs fold in snugly to protect its head and neck. If the young turtle doesn't move, its color and pattern help it blend in with the ground. An enemy might not see the camouflaged hatchling. With some luck, these new gopher tortoises will survive for forty years or more as they grow to be the size of basketballs.

A FUTURE FOR BABY REPTILES?

Life is hard for animal babies of all kinds, but for young reptiles, surviving their first years is especially difficult. Even though they are born with all the instincts they will ever need, most baby reptiles do not survive the many dangers in their lives.

Sadly, people are one of the biggest threats to reptiles. The quiet, shy reptiles are among the most feared and misunderstood of all animals. Without realizing how important reptiles are in nature, people often destroy them on sight. People also have taken over and changed forests, swamps, and other reptile living spaces. The animals are rapidly being crowded out of their habitats.

Wildlife experts have become concerned about the future of many snakes, lizards, turtles, and crocodilians. Zoos all over the world are trying to breed those animals that are close to becoming extinct. Newborn reptiles that have been cared for in captivity and then released have a much better chance of surviving their first year than those born in the wild. Other organizations are also trying to protect reptiles and their natural habitats.

It is important for people to learn respect for the lives and needs of reptiles and other wild animals. Understanding the value of these creatures in the balance of nature can make the earth a better place for people and for the animals.

This baby loggerhead sea turtle, hatched in captivity, is released on a quiet southern beach.

GLOSSARY

Burrow—a tunnel or underground home.

Camouflage—color and patterns in an animal's body covering that help the animal blend in with its surroundings.

Crocodilian—a kind of large reptile found in warm waters of the world; crocodilians have four legs and a powerful tail for swimming.

Egg tooth—a horny tip on the upper part of a hatching reptile's jaw that helps it escape from the eggshell.

Habitat—a place where plants and animals live naturally.

Hatchling—an animal that has just come out of its eggshell.

Incubate—to warm an egg so the young inside will develop and hatch.

Predator—an animal that kills other animals for its food.

Prehensile tail—a tail adapted for grasping or holding.

Prey—an animal killed and eaten by another animal.

Rain forest—a type of forest rich in plant and animal life that is kept green year round by high rainfall and mild temperatures.

Reptile—any of a group of animals that have scale-covered bodies and breathe by using lungs.

Scales—dry, horny plates covering the body of a reptile.

Scutes—enlarged scales, such as those found on the belly of a snake and the shell of a turtle.

Spectacle scale—a clear, round scale covering the eye of a snake.

Tortoise—a land turtle usually having thick legs and a high-domed shell.

Venom—a poison made in an animal's body.

Vent—an opening in a reptile's body where eggs, young, or waste materials are passed to the outside.

Yolk—food material inside an egg used by the developing baby.

INDEX

Photographs are in **boldface**.